RIHANNA

PHOTOGRAPHY AND CONCEPT BY
SIMON HENWOOD

RIZZOLI
NEW YORK

New York · Paris · London · Milan

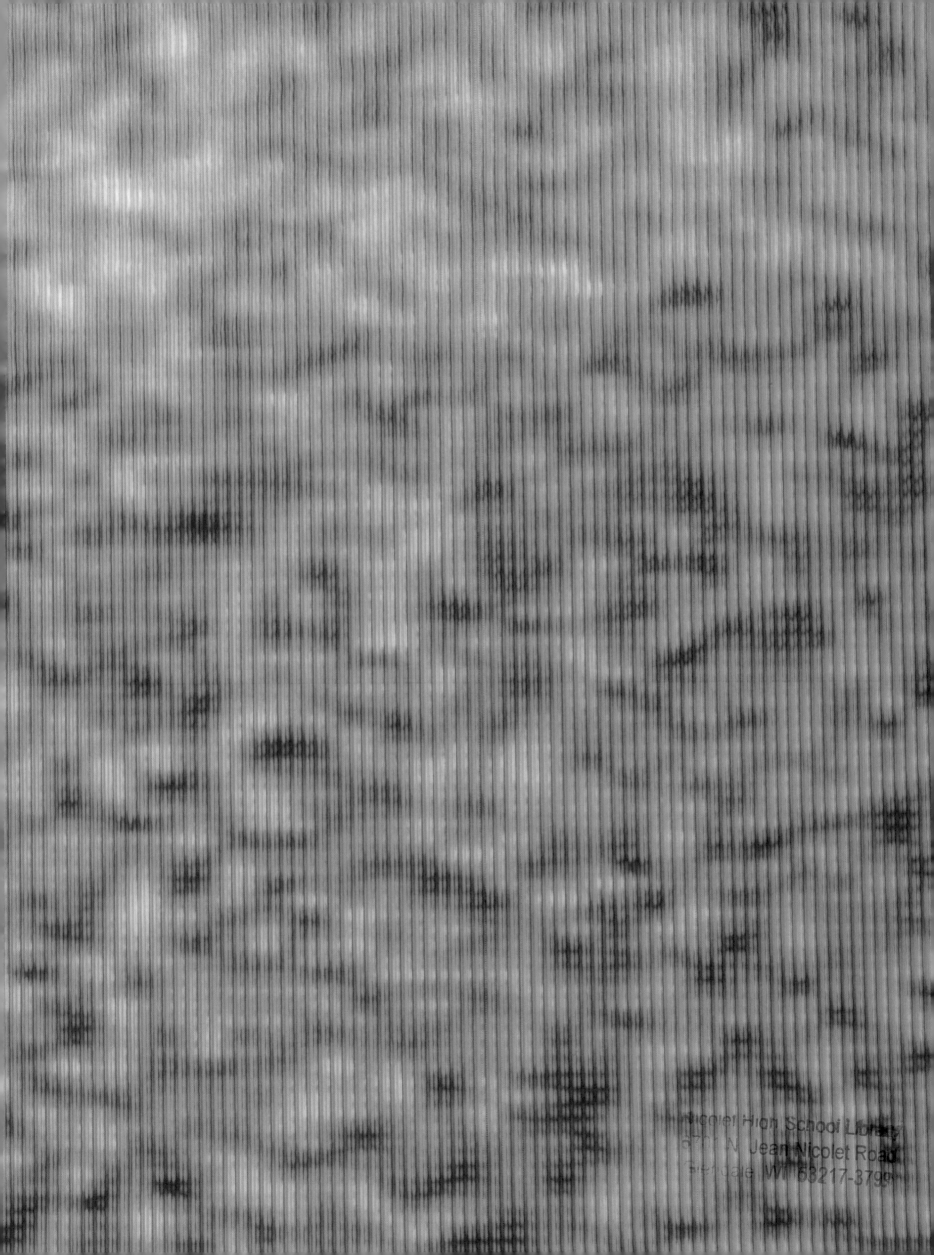

First published in the United States of America in 2010

by Rizzoli International Publications, Inc.

300 Park Avenue South

New York, New York 10010

www.rizzoliusa.com

© 2010 Robyn Rihanna Fenty c/o Rebel-One Management

Photographs and Introduction © 2010 Simon Henwood with the exception of pages 13, 27, and 29 photographs © Ellen von Unwerth

Foreword © 2010 Alexandre Vauthier

Design by Simon Henwood and Jesse Richards
Edited by Leah Whisler

2010 2011 2012 2013 2014 / 10 9 8 7 6 5 4 3 2 1

Printed in China

Library of Congress Catalog Control Number: 2009943978

Paperback ISBN: 978-0-8478-3510-2

Hardcover ISBN: 978-0-8478-3511-9

Deluxe ISBN: 978-0-8478-3632-1

www.rihannanow.com

MADE WITH
SWAROVSKI
ELEMENTS

Deluxe Clamshell made with SWAROVSKI ELEMENTS
SWAROVSKI® is a registered trademark.

PREFACE

THERE ARE UNFORGETTABLE ENCOUNTERS
IN LIFE: MY ENCOUNTER WITH RIHANNA
WILL BE ENGRAVED IN MY MEMORY
FOREVER.

BEAUTIFUL, CHARISMATIC, RISK-TAKER,
CREATIVE, AND BLESSED WITH AN
OUTSTANDING AESTHETIC MATURITY, SHE
IS A CATALYST FOR INSPIRATION.

BEYOND HER INCREDIBLE ARTISTIC
TALENT, SHE HAS AN INDEFINABLE AURA
THAT MESMERIZES, THAT FASCINATES:
THE KIND OF AURA THAT MAKES ONE BE.

IT IS NOT MY CLOTHING THAT
HIGHLIGHTS HER BEAUTY, BUT RATHER
SHE, WITH HER INCREDIBLE
PERSONALITY, WHO GIVES REAL MEANING
TO MY CLOTHING. SHE IS ALREADY A
GREAT STAR, BUT FROM THIS MERE
OBSERVATION, I CONFIRM SHE'S YET A
TRUE MUSIC ICON.

SO IT IS USELESS TO WONDER WHETHER
I AM HAPPY TO PARTICIPATE IN HER
ADVENTURE: I FEEL TOTALLY BLESSED.

ALEXANDRE VAUTHIER

INTRODUCTION

AT THE TIME OF THIS WRITING, WE ARE IN FULL PRODUCTION REHEARSALS ON RIHANNA'S FIRST HEADLINE WORLD TOUR. AS HER CREATIVE DIRECTOR, I HAVE BEEN WITH HER FOR THE LAST NINE MONTHS, PREPARING FOR THESE FINAL MOMENTS. LAST GIRL ON EARTH WILL DEBUT IN LESS THAN A MONTH IN THE BELGIAN CITY OF ANTWERP, HOME TO DESIGNER MARTIN MARGIELA.

THE JOURNEY BEGAN LAST YEAR AT THE PARIS FASHION SHOWS, WHERE RIHANNA CAUSED QUITE A STIR—TO THE POINT THAT DESIGNERS WERE TURNING AWAY CELEBRITIES FROM THEIR FRONT ROWS— SHE SAT ALONE, AN EXCEPTION AMONG THE REGULAR FASHION CROWD. FOR HER EFFORTLESS STYLE SHE SHONE OUT IN THE MIDST OF THE "TRYING TOO HARDS."

THE PAPARAZZI FOLLOWED RELENTLESSLY, USUALLY IN A CONVOY OF SCOOTERS, BUT SHE NEVER SEEMED FAZED. HER MIND ALWAYS REMAINED ON THE JOB, ALWAYS EXCITED TO SEE FANTASTIC NEW CLOTHES—LIKE ANY YOUNG GIRL THRILLED TO BE THERE—AND BE ONE OF THE FIRST TO SEE IT ALL. WE ALWAYS CALLED PEOPLE STRAIGHT AFTER A SHOW IN THE CAR, AND WENT INTO ALL KINDS OF FRENZIES TRYING TO SECURE NEW PIECES BEFORE THEY WERE SNAPPED UP.

THEN, SLOWLY, THE CLOTHES STARTED TO ARRIVE, FRESHLY PICKED FROM THE CATWALK FOR THE RATED R ALBUM SHOOT THE NEXT WEEK IN BERLIN. AS THE WEEK PROGRESSED, EVERYTHING BECAME MORE INTENSE—SOMETIMES SIX SHOWS A DAY, FITTINGS, PRESS, AND LATE NIGHTS IN THE RECORDING STUDIO FINISHING THE ALBUM. I REMEMBER ONE NIGHT SITTING UP WITH HER UNTIL THE WEE HOURS AS SHE DREW, MADE DIAGRAMS, AND WROTE OUT LYRICS FOR THE ALBUM BOOKLET. I ALWAYS JOKE, "WAITING FOR RIHANNA," (OR "WAIT YOUR TURN," MORE APPROPRIATELY) BUT SHE WORKS HARDER THAN ANYONE I KNOW ON SO MANY LEVELS—ALWAYS WITH A RELAXED BARBADIAN STRIDE, AND ALWAYS WITH TIME FOR A PASSING FAN ENCOUNTER OR TWO.

NEXT, WE MEET WITH ELLEN VON UNWERTH IN BERLIN FOR THE ALBUM SHOOT. TWENTY-SIX SETUPS IN TWO DAYS—A MOUNTAIN-SIZED WARDROBE, DOZENS OF MANNEQUIN DUMMIES, A BABY PANTHER, AND STACKS OF THE SIGNATURE TVS BURNING STATIC IN EVERY ROOM. FOR THE FIRST TIME, WE ARE IN THE WORLD OF LAST GIRL ON EARTH, THE FOUNDATIONS OF THE CONCEPT THAT WILL COME ALIVE ON THE STAGE IN TEN MONTH'S TIME.

THE ATMOSPHERE IN BERLIN IS PERFECT— THE OLD RUINS OF CITIES PAST STILL POURING THROUGH ITS REFURBISHMENT. THERE ARE NO GLOSSY APARTMENT SHOOTS OR SHINY POSSESSIONS—JUST THE RAW BONES OF AN EMPTY WAREHOUSE SET DISTINGUISHED AS A POST-APOCALYPTIC EMPTY WORLD FOR HER TO COMMAND. ELLEN MAKES IT SEXY, OF COURSE—IN THAT DARK CHEEKY WAY THAT HER FASHION APPEALS TO HOT-BLOODED MEN AS WELL. RIHANNA HAS STUDIED EVERY PHOTO ELLEN EVER TOOK AND KNOWS EXACTLY WHAT SHE WANTS FROM HER PHOTOGRAPHER. THE BOTH OF THEM ARE IN HEAVEN FOR TWO DAYS.

A FEW WEEKS LATER, RATED R IS RELEASED TO CRITICAL ACCLAIM. HER MOST PERSONAL RECORD TO DATE AND A BIG GAMBLE IN SOME RESPECTS, IT EXPLODES WITH SUCCESS, EVEN WITHOUT HER NAME ON THE COVER— REPLACED WITH THE NOW ICONIC R LOGO, WHICH I DESIGNED OUT OF A BEER COASTER LATE ONE NIGHT IN A LONDON PUB. SHE IS NOW OFFICIALLY A BIGGER STAR THAN ANYONE KNEW.

THE PICTURES IN THIS BOOK WERE TAKEN AS WE TRAVELED AROUND TOGETHER, AND I THINK THEY SHOW SOMETHING NEW OF HER—THE REAL GIRL WORKING AND HAVING FUN DOING IT. RIHANNA WANTED HER ADMIRERS TO SEE HER IN THIS WAY. FOR ME, THE PHOTOGRAPHS FORM A PORTRAIT OF A REMARKABLE YOUNG WOMAN—STILL JUST TWENTY-ONE FOR MOST OF THEM, BUT CLEARLY WISE BEYOND HER YEARS AND AS SWEET AND UNAFFECTED AS ANY GIRL OR FAN HER AGE.

NOW, HERE IN L.A. AS I SHAPE THE SHOW WITH JAMIE KING AND ALL THE INCREDIBLE CHOREOGRAPHERS, LIGHTING DESIGNERS, STYLISTS, DANCERS, AND CREW—THE VISION OF LAST GIRL ON EARTH IS BEING BORN TO NEW HEIGHTS AND DEPTHS. FROM ITS HUMBLE BEGINNINGS—RIHANNA'S NEW WORLD HAS GROWN INTO SOMETHING THAT WILL ASTONISH AND DAZZLE LIKE THE STAR HERSELF.

SIMON HENWOOD

LAST GIRL ON EARTH

LAST GIRL ON EARTH WAS INSPIRED BY APOCALYPTIC MOVIES SUCH AS *THE OMEGA MAN* AND, MOST RECENTLY, ITS REMAKE, *I AM LEGEND*.

THE IDEA WAS TO CREATE FOR RIHANNA A WORLD OF HER OWN. I HAD ALSO RECENTLY RE-READ URSULA K. LE GUIN'S BOOK, *THE LATHE OF HEAVEN* IN WHICH THE DREAMS OF A GIFTED VISIONARY BECOME REALITY—AND SOMETIMES WITH CATACLYSMIC CONSEQUENCES. THE TWO STORY LINES COMBINED BECAME A GREAT SOURCE FOR HER NARRATIVE.

RIHANNA DREAMS OF A WORLD OF HER OWN—WHEN SHE WAKES, THE WORLD IS AN ABANDONED SHRINE TO HERSELF. EVERY MAGAZINE COVER, BILLBOARD, AND TV BROADCAST IS DEVOTED TO HER. THE "R" SYMBOL TAKES ON MANY ROLES IN THIS BACKDROP—A LITTLE LIKE THE "V" SIGN FROM THE TV SHOW—IT APPEARS CARVED IN WALLS, GRAFFITIED, ON GIANT VEGAS-STYLE SIGNS IN FRONT OF AN ABANDONED STADIUM, AND BURNING OUT OF THE STATIC OF OLD TELEVISION SETS.

R Logo

The "R" logo started as a piece of origami—a little folded piece of paper I then worked up into a CGI model. I wanted to create something that could work on multiple levels. The final design has been used across the campaign for Rihanna's tour—from the website as an animation sting to jewelry design to the print logo used on *Rated R* and tour posters.

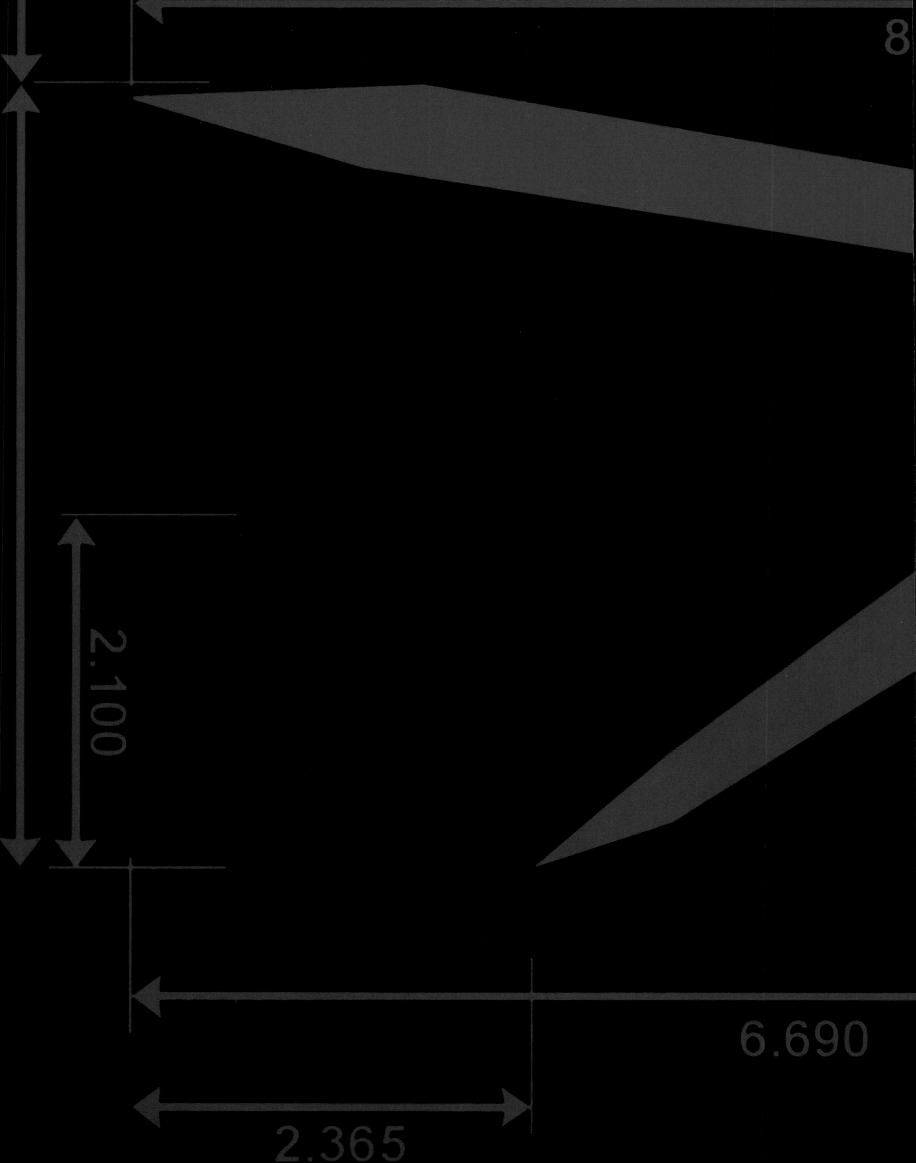

2.100

6.690

2.365

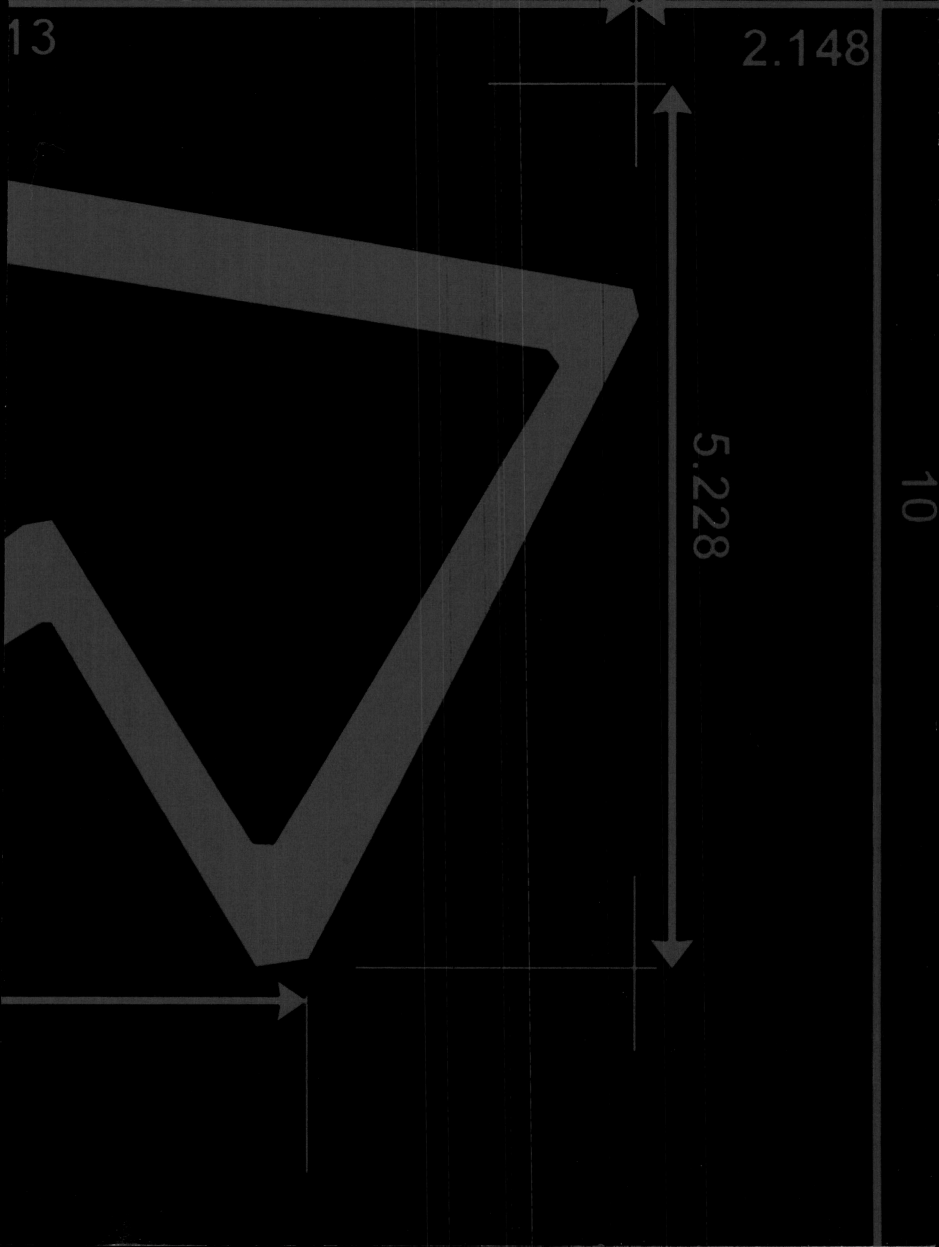

FIRST STOP BERLIN

THE FIRST PART OF OUR CREATIVE JOURNEY TOOK US TO BERLIN.

HERE WE MET WITH GERMAN PHOTOGRAPHER ELLEN VON UNWERTH TO DISCUSS IDEAS FOR THE ALBUM SHOOT.

ELLEN HAD PHOTOGRAPHED RIHANNA A FEW YEARS AGO AND WOULD BE GREAT AT CAPTURING A MORE INTIMATE SIDE OF THE STAR FOR THIS VERY PERSONAL ALBUM.

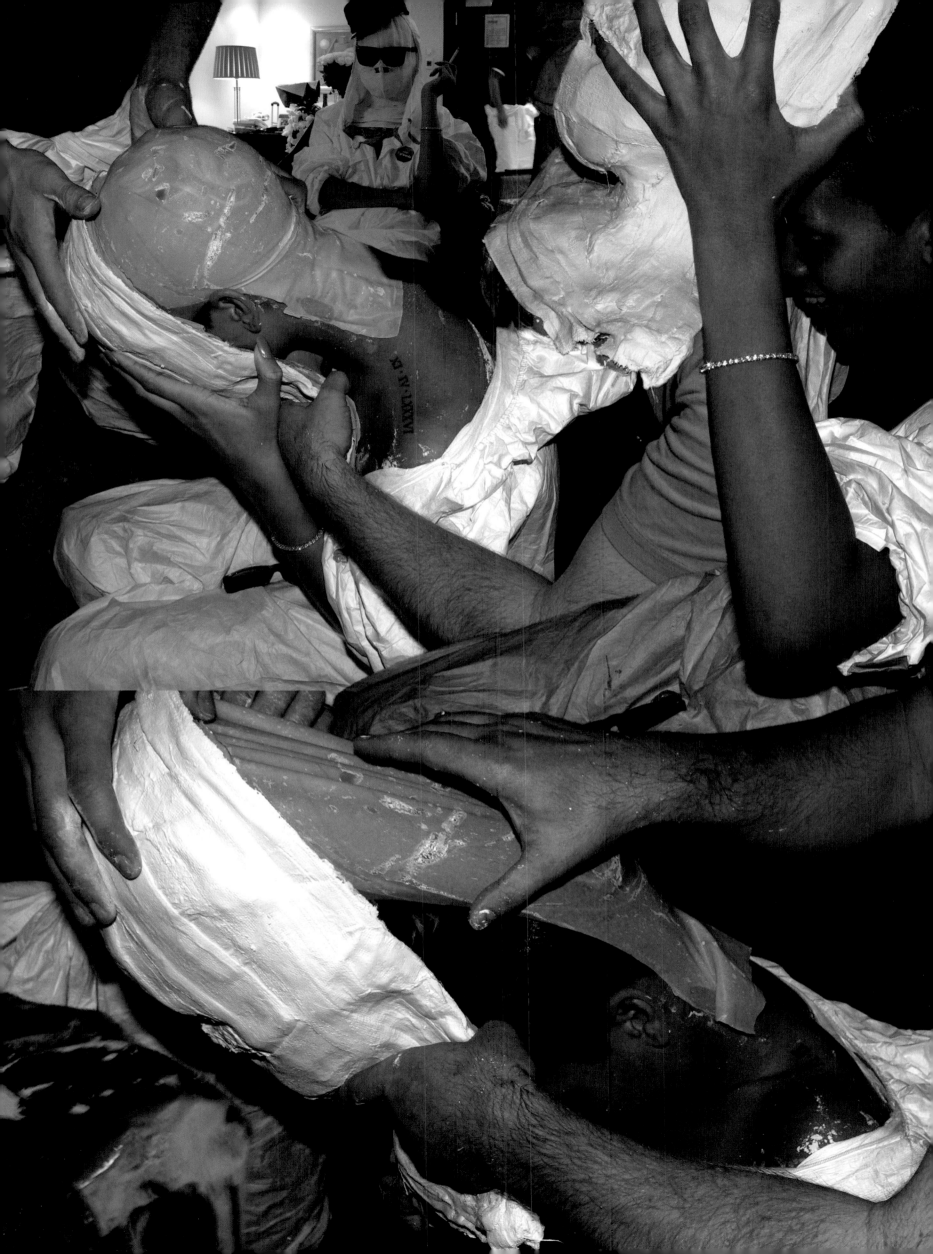

PLASTERED IN PARIS

DURING PARIS FASHION WEEK, WE TURNED RIHANNA'S HOTEL ROOM INTO A CASTING SUITE, LITERALLY.

THE PROCESS OF APPLYING THE SILICON, THEN THE PLASTER ON TOP, PIECE BY PIECE, TOOK A COUPLE OF HOURS DURING WHICH SHE HAD TO REMAIN COMPLETELY STILL.

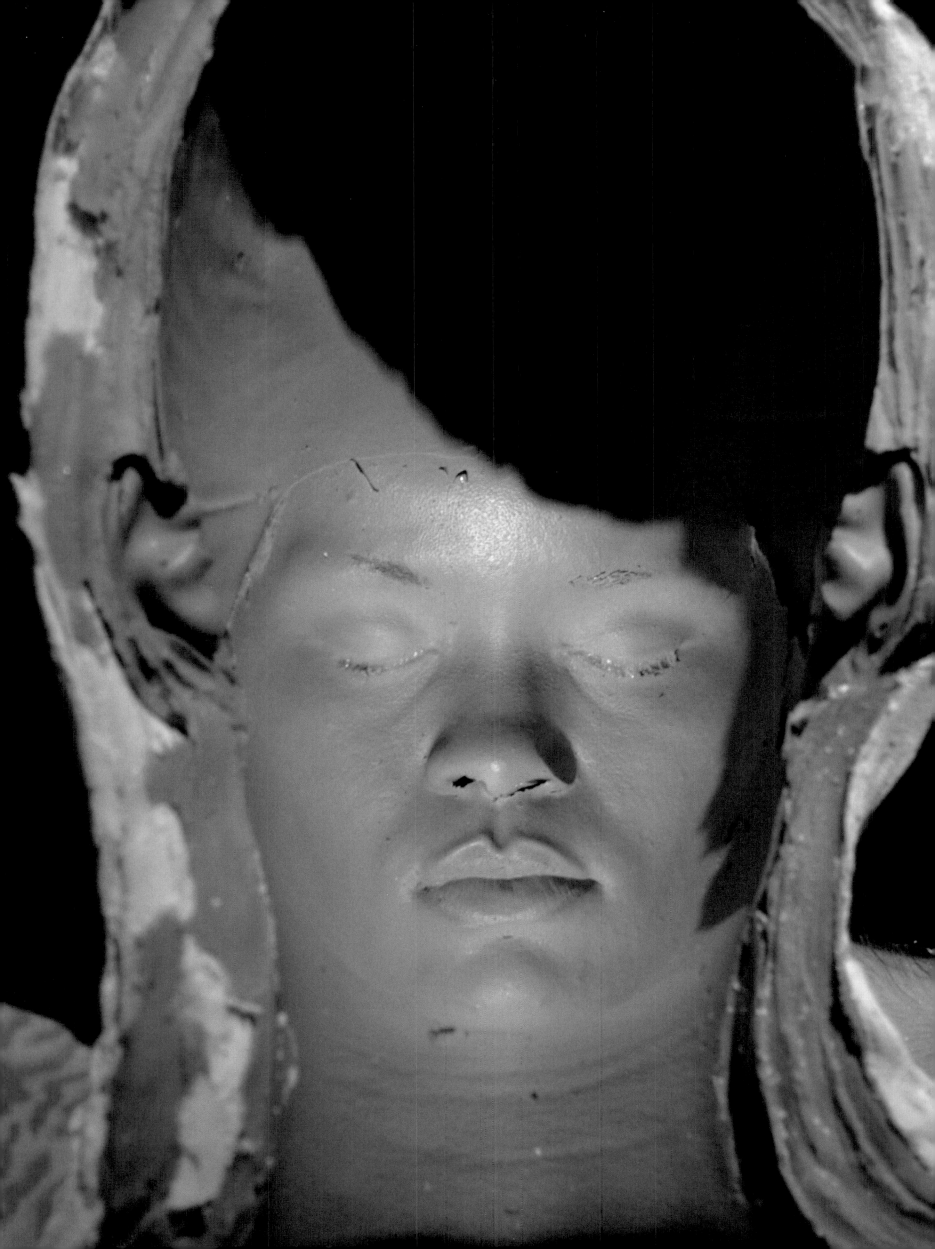

MODER

PEOPLE WERE CAPTIVATED BY RIHANNA DURING PARIS FASHION WEEK. SOME SIMPLY STARED AS IF SHE WAS AN ALIEN. PEOPLE WOULD COME UP AND GUSH ABOUT HER LOOKING LIKE A PERFECT DOLL OR SOME OTHER PARISIAN FANTASY.

SOMETIMES I WOULD STAND AWAY AND OBSERVE THE SCENE, GET A BIGGER PICTURE. ALWAYS I SAW THIS YOUNG GIRL TOTALLY COMPOSED AND SERENE IN A TORNADO OF MADNESS.

RIHANNA'S SECURITY GUARD TOLD ME JEAN PAUL GAULTIER SHOWED HIM AROUND THE VENUE OF HIS SHOW BEFOREHAND TO PERSONALLY ENSURE HER SAFETY. THERE WERE EXTRAORDINARY THINGS HAPPENING THAT WEEK.

L'atelier du Glamour

FITTINGS

THERE WERE CLOTHES FLYING IN TO PARIS FROM EVERYWHERE — READY TO SHIP TO BERLIN FOR THE ALBUM SHOOT. EACH NIGHT AFTER THE FASHION SHOWS WE HAD FITTINGS — SOME FOR THE SHOOT AND SOME FOR THE NEXT DAY'S APPEARANCES. IT WAS A CONSTANT CONVEYER BELT OF LOVE!, HATE!, AND MAYBE.

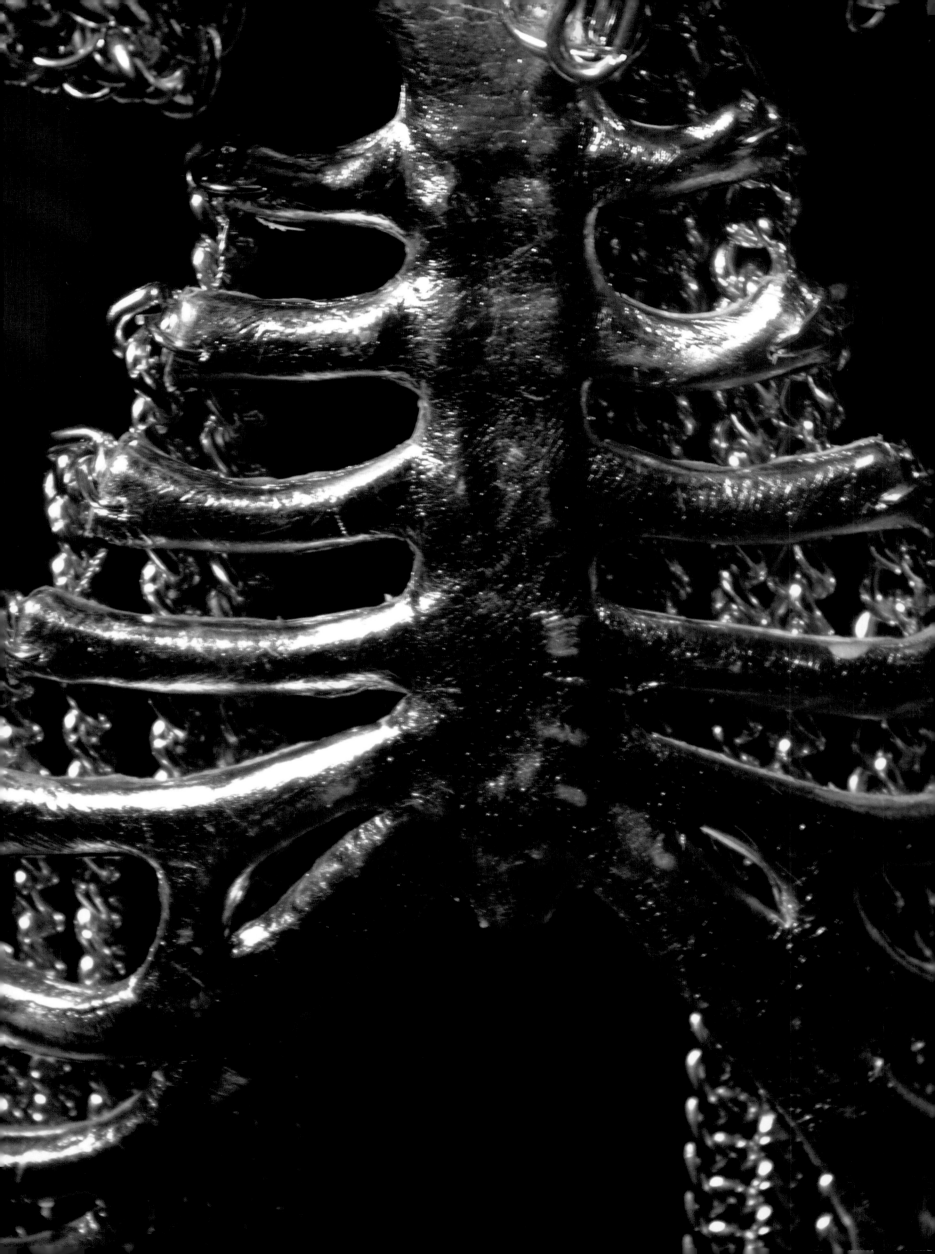

RATED R

RATED R ALBUM SHOOT

THIS IS OUTSIDE CENTRAL STATION IN BERLIN WITH ELLEN VON UNWERTH AS WE BEGAN SHOOTING FOR RIHANNA'S ALBUM, *RATED R*. THE PAPARAZZI TURNED UP, SO WE HAD TO CREATE BARRIERS AROUND THE SHOOT TO STOP THEM FROM GETTING PICTURES. UNFORTUNATELY, THE SHOOT WAS ALL OVER THE NET WITHIN THE HOUR. WE NEVER USED THE SETUP IN THE END.

MANNEQUINS AND BARBIES

ONE OF THE LOCATIONS FOR THE ALBUM SHOOT IN BERLIN WAS AN OLD BEER HOPS FACTORY. IT HAD BEEN EMPTY FOR TEN YEARS, BUT STILL REEKED OF SOMETHING UNHOLY. WE DISCOVERED AN UNDERGROUND CONCRETE BUNKER THERE. WE FILLED IT WITH OLD TVS AND EERIE MANNEQUINS. THEY LOOKED LIKE THEY HAD ALWAYS BEEN THERE. AGAIN, THE SHOOT WAS NEVER USED.

AT TIMES THE SHOP DUMMIES SEEMED TO BE EVERYWHERE WATCHING US. EVEN DECAPITATED OR LIMBLESS THEY HAD AN INCREDIBLE PRESENCE. ONCE YOU START RESEARCHING THEM YOU FIND THERE ARE HUNDREDS OF DESIGNS. THE OLDER DESIGNS WERE THE BEST AND BASED ON REAL MODELS.

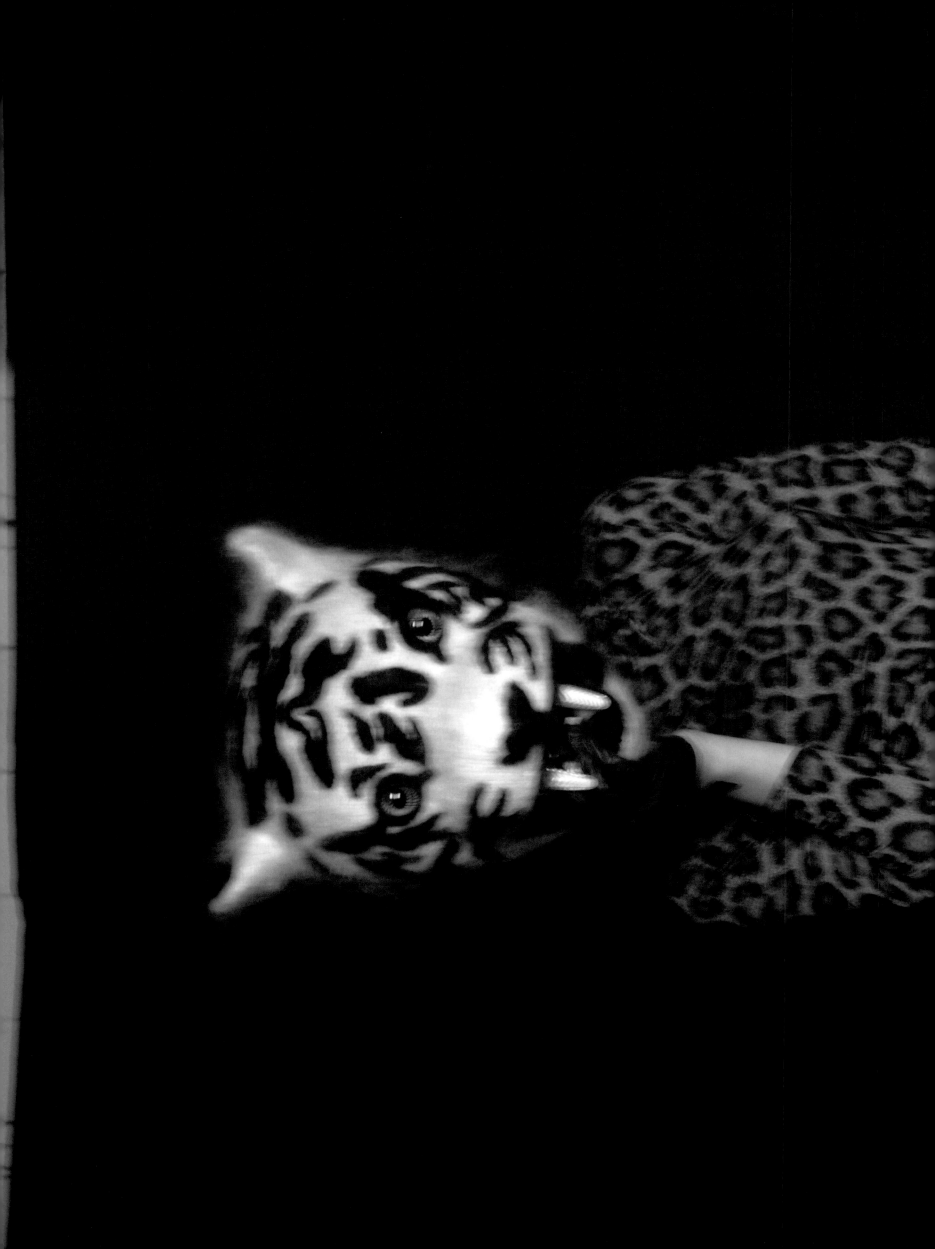

STATIC TVS

ONE OF THE SIGNATURE IMAGES OF THE CAMPAIGN IS THE BURNING STATIC WALLS OF TVS. THEY WERE A BACKDROP THAT ALWAYS CONVEYED RADIO SILENCE — THAT THERE WAS AN EMPTY WORLD OUTSIDE THE ROOM. THE LIGHT THAT THEY GAVE OUT WAS GHOSTLY, TOO, AND EVEN IN A ROOM FULL OF THE PRODUCTION CREW, YOU COULD NOT HELP BUT FEEL SOMEHOW LONELY IN THEIR PRESENCE.

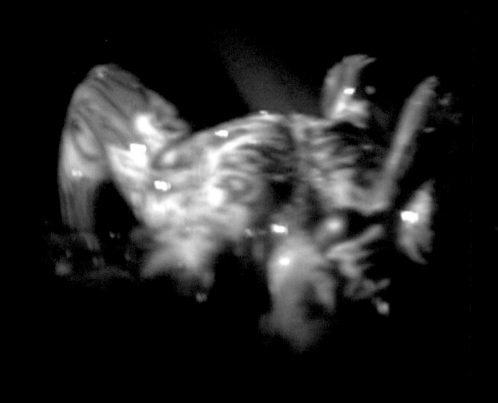

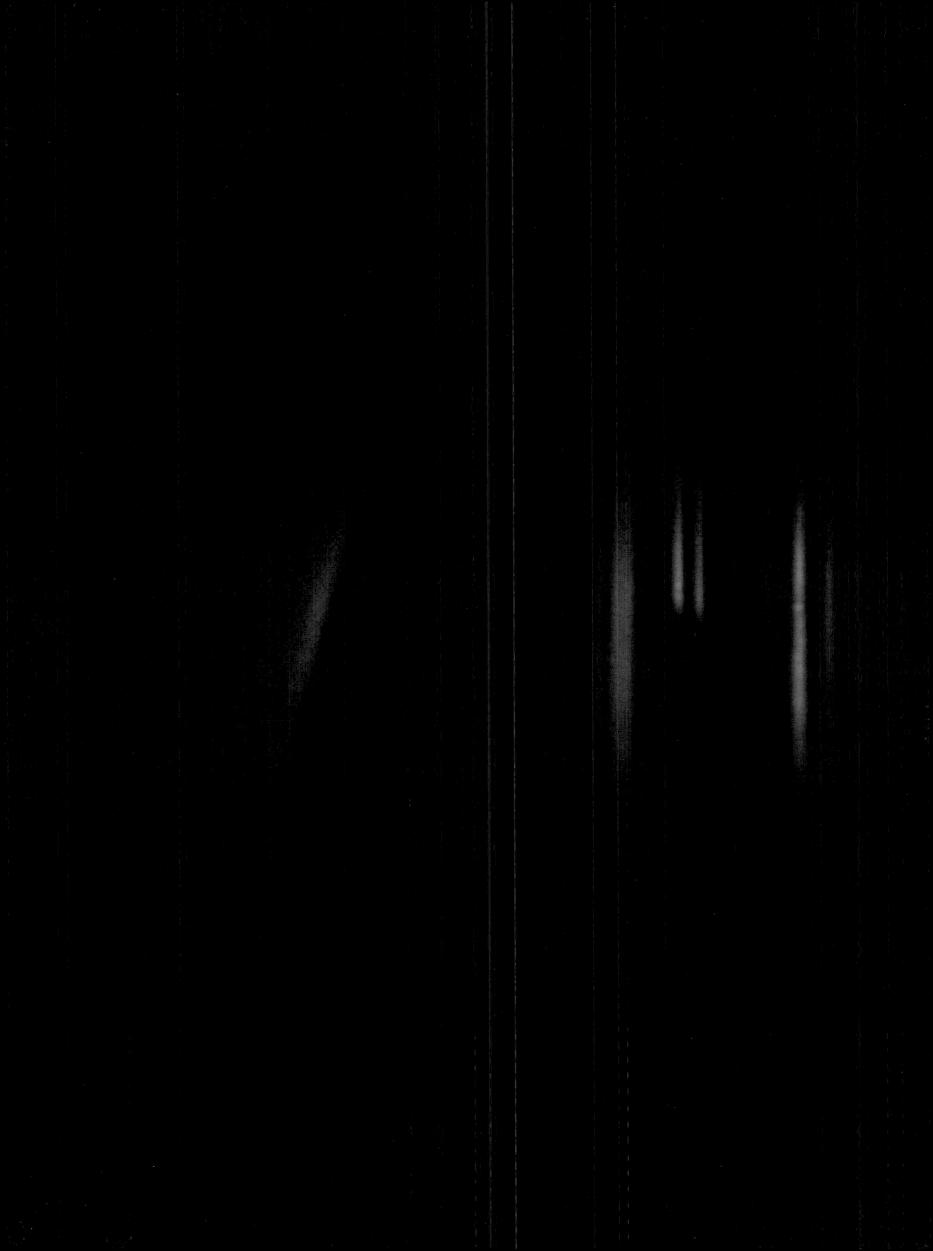

LASER DRESS

THIS IS THE INCREDIBLE LASER
DRESS THAT STARTED IT ALL.

I SPENT SEVERAL MONTHS
NEGOTIATING WITH HUSSEIN
CHALAYAN TO BORROW THIS. IT IS
AN ACTUAL MUSEUM PIECE HOUSED
IN THE VICTORIA & ALBERT MUSEUM
IN LONDON AND IS VERY FRAGILE.

THIS WAS THE LAST SETUP OF THE
ALBUM SHOOT.

STUDIO R

AMERICAN MUSIC AWARDS

RIHANNA WAS RUNNING BEHIND WHEN WE SHOT THE OPENING VIDEO FOR THE AMERICAN MUSIC AWARDS, BUT LUCKILY I WAS PREPARED. I HAD SHOT THE WHOLE VIDEO WITH A BODY DOUBLE FIRST AND EVEN HAD TIME TO DO SOME EDITING BEFORE SHE ARRIVED.

AT MIDNIGHT, I SHOWED HER THE CUT, WHICH SHE LOVED, THEN SHOT HER CLOSE-UPS IN THIRTY MINUTES.

THE VIDEO WAS DELIVERED A FEW HOURS LATER.

L.A. Rock Star

These pictures were
taken during the last week
of production rehearsals for
the tour.

Every day new elements were
added to the show—Staging,
costumes, animation, and
lighting design—everything
began to take shape.

You never knew what was
going to turn up each day
when you entered the
soundstage.

LIVE R

LAST GIRL ON EARTH

THE FOLLOWING ARE SHOTS
TAKEN AS LAST GIRL ON EARTH
WENT LIVE.

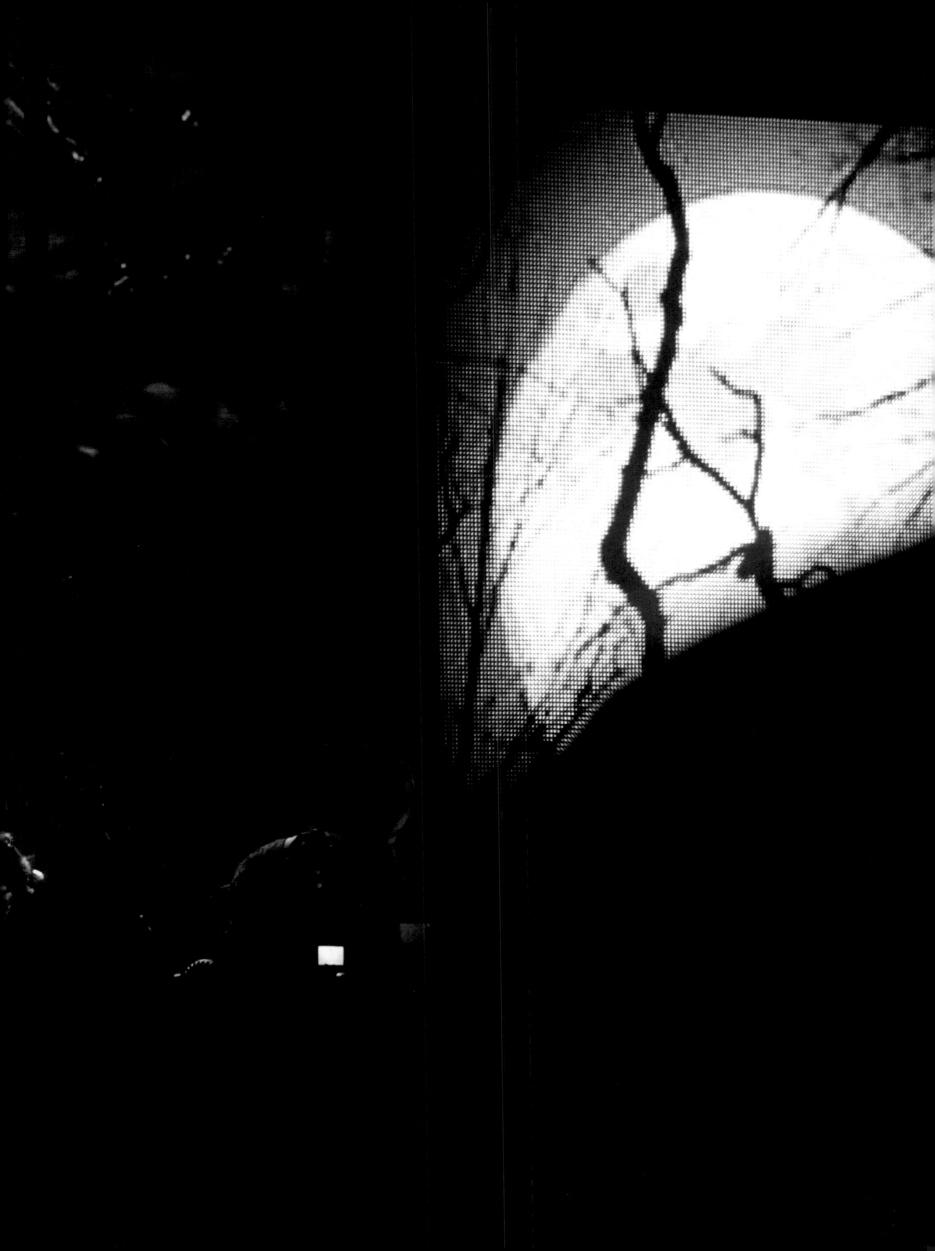

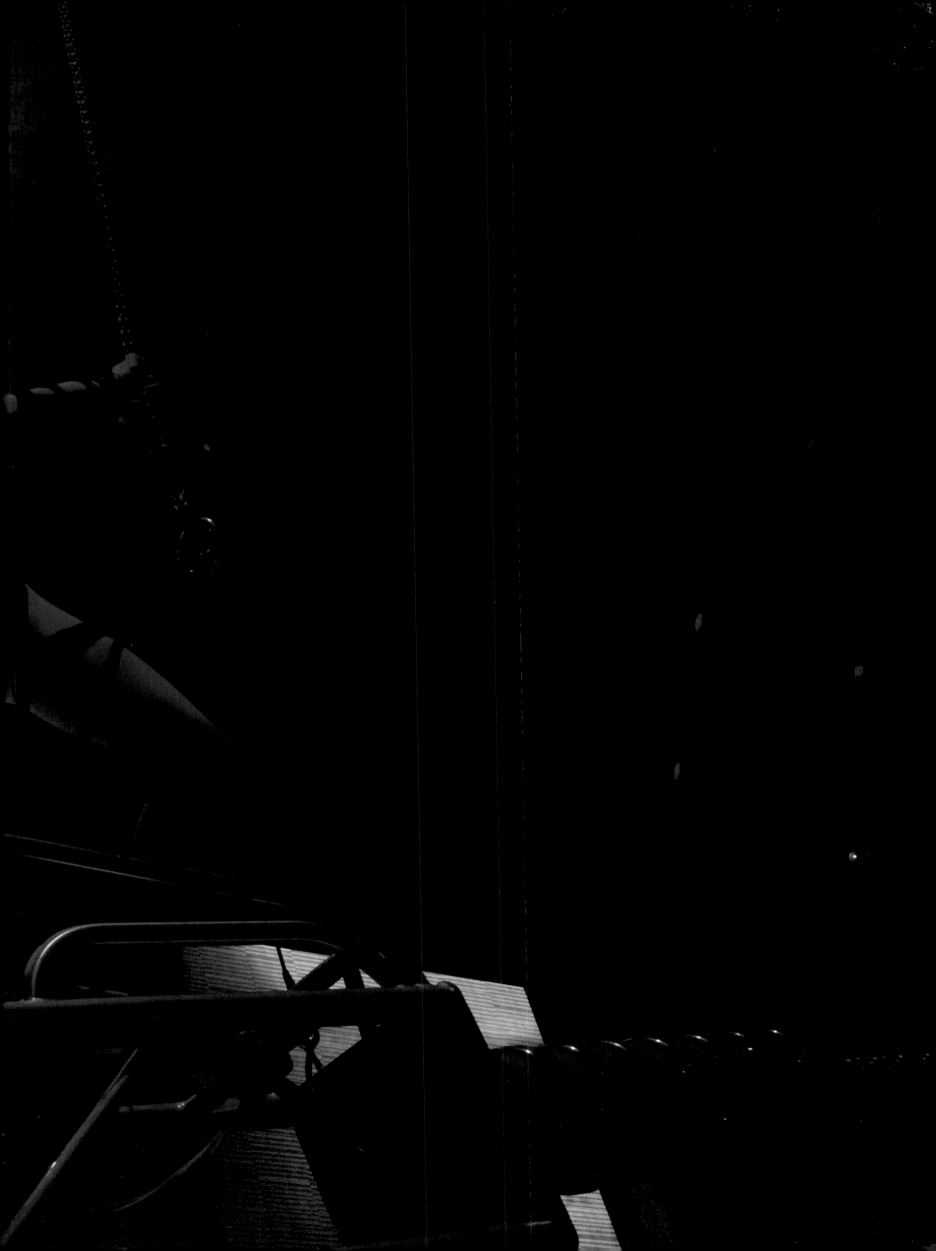

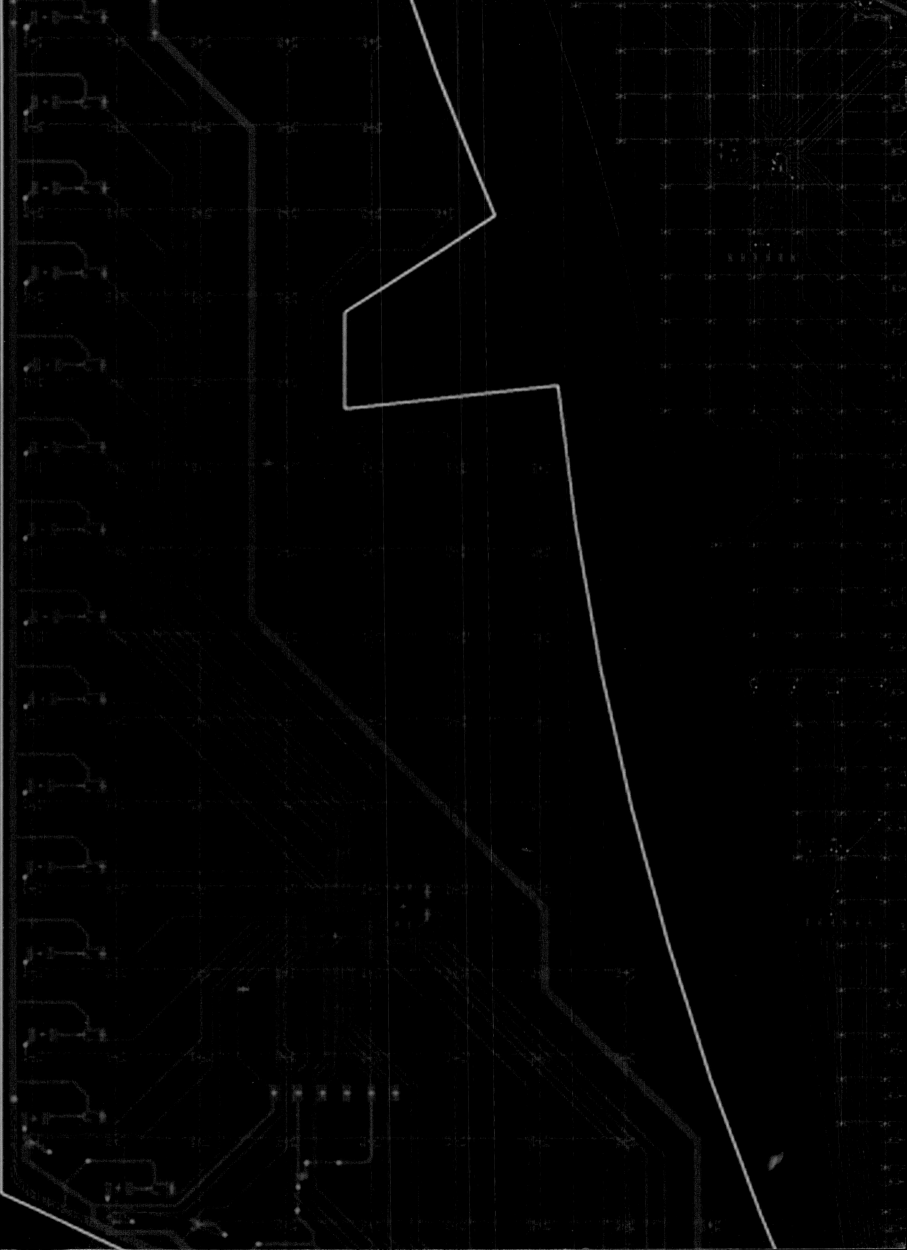

SUCH A FUCKING LADY